*A book
is a present you can open
again and again.*

THIS BOOK BELONGS TO

_____

FROM

_____

# WONDER WHY

# All About You

with Inspector McQ

Written by Patty Rutland Mullins
Illustrated by Joan Holub

World Book, Inc.
a Scott Fetzer company
Chicago London Sydney Toronto

Copyright © 1992
World Book, Inc.
525 West Monroe Street
Chicago, Illinois 60661

Printed in the United States of America
ISBN 0-7166-1612-2
Library of Congress Catalog Card No. 91-65494

8 9 10 11 12 13 14 15 99 98 97 96


Cover design by Rosa Cabrera
Book design by Ann Tomasic
Inspector McQ illustrated by Eileen Mueller Neill

# Hello. My name is Inspector McQuestion (McQ for short) and my job today is to find out facts about the amazing human body.

Have you ever wondered why you are growing or what causes dreams? I was investigating questions such as these and came up with so many interesting answers! Come along. Let's find out more about you.

# Why are you growing?

You know how to make a building out of blocks. First, you plan what you want. Then you follow your plan, adding one block at a time.

Did you know you are made of "building blocks," too? These blocks are called "cells." They do not look like the blocks you play with, and they are too tiny to see with your eyes.

With a microscope you could see how cells are shaped. A microscope makes small things look big, so we can study them. That dot in the middle of each cell is the control center. There is a plan just for you in that control center, something like a secret code.

You begin as one cell. The plan in the first cell decides almost everything about you: how tall you will be, what you will look like, and more. One cell turns into more and more, and more. We say it *multiplies*. You keep growing because your cells keep making more cells. When you are fully grown, you will be made of trillions of cells. That's a lot of blocks!

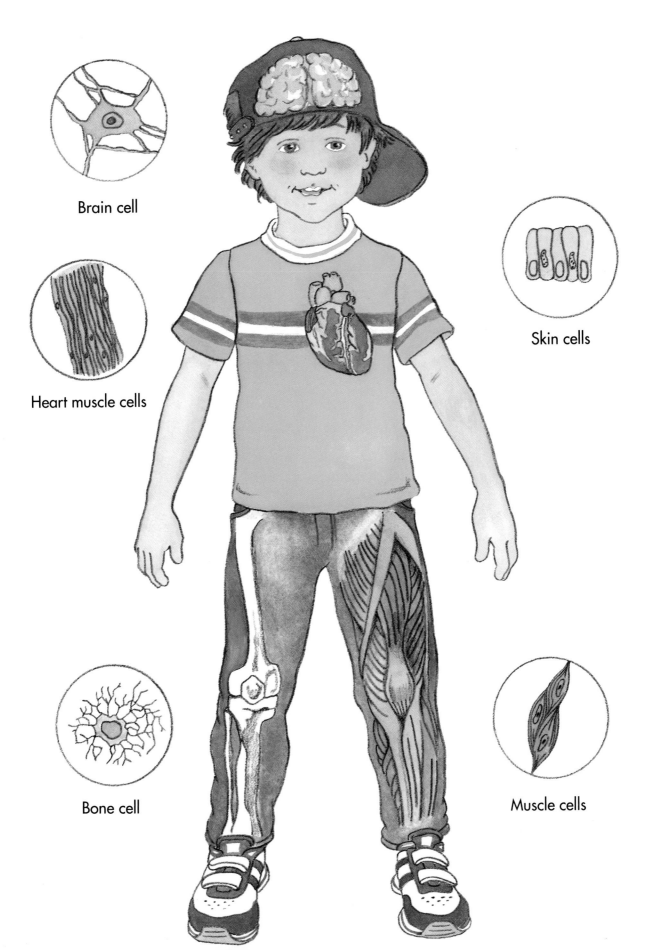

Brain cell

Heart muscle cells

Skin cells

Bone cell

Muscle cells

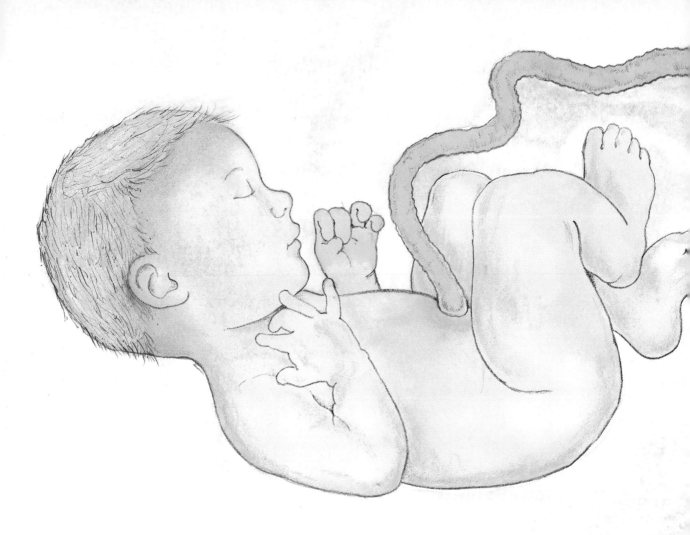

# *Why do you have a bellybutton*

I imagine you were surprised when you first noticed that circle in the middle of your tummy. Did you wonder what it was?

Of course, your bellybutton is not really a "button" at all. Its official name is "navel," and before you were born, it had a very important purpose. Even when you were a tiny baby, living inside your mother, you needed to be fed. Your mother could not reach you with her hands, so something else happened.

A special cord, called an umbilical cord, formed. It was attached to the place where you were growing, and to the middle of your tummy. When your mother ate, some of her nutrition and oxygen made its way to you through the cord. You can think of the umbilical cord as a lifeline you shared with your mother.

When you were born, the cord was cut. The place where it was cut dried into a round little folded spot that you've had ever since.

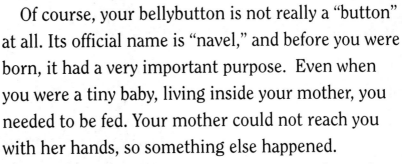

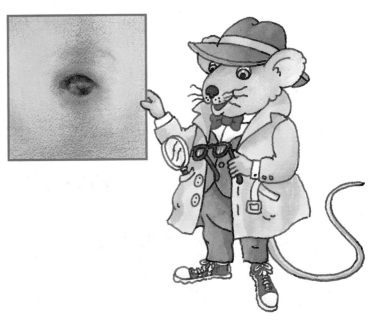

# Where do freckles come from ?

Out with your secret, my fine freckled friends! Where do those dots come from?

Actually, freckles are not really a secret. After a little searching for the answer, here is what I found out: Everyone's skin has a special brown coloring called melanin. You were born with a lot of melanin or perhaps just a little. Suppose the melanin builds up in small patches on your skin. These are freckles—the small patches of melanin.

Scientists think that sunlight may help to darken the melanin spots and make more freckles. Since I don't have freckles, I can't be sure about what sunlight does. If you or a friend have freckles, be a detective and see what happens. See if more freckles appear when you're playing outside a lot, especially in summer.

# Why doesn't it hurt to cut hair ?

W hich feels better—getting a haircut or combing your hair when it's messy or snarly? Quite a puzzle, isn't it? Pulling hair hurts, but cutting hair doesn't hurt. Let's find out why.

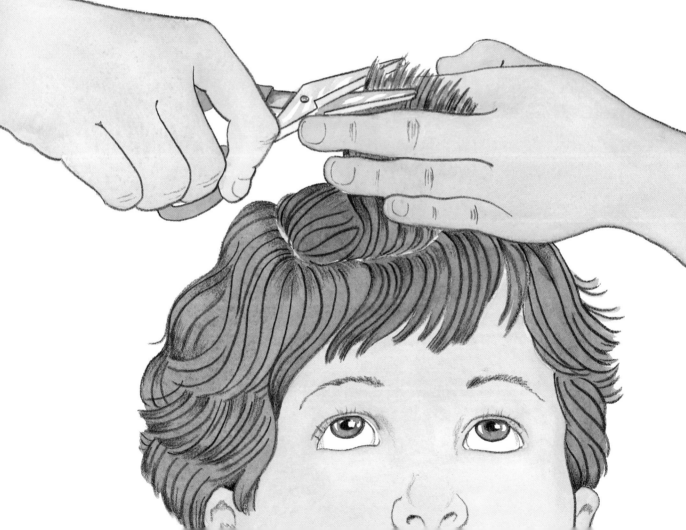

Root

Under a microscope, you could see that a strand of hair has different parts. On the outside part, called the cuticle, crusty flaps overlap like fish scales. On the inside, we find a hard material called the cortex.

What we do not find in the strand of hair are nerve cells. Nerve cells, those that help you feel, send messages to your brain, such as "It hurts!"

The roots of your hair, just inside your scalp, do have nerve cells. Combing or pulling hair tugs on these nerves, which then send "ouch" messages to the brain. Since the hair strands are outside your scalp, away from the nerve cells, they cannot send "ouch" messages. A good thing, I say! Otherwise, no one would ever want to get a haircut.

# Why is hair curly or straight ?

Inspectors have to look their best. I comb my hair every day. It's so straight, and yet some folks have curly or wavy hair. Why is this?

In a way, hair type is like skin color and freckles: these kinds of qualities are passed on to you from other members of your family.

Close up, with a microscope, you could see that hairs have different forms. The form gives a clue as to whether the hair is straight, curly, or wavy. Strands of straight hair look like pieces of uncooked spaghetti, all in a row. The ends look perfectly round.

Under the microscope, curly strands look flat, like pieces of ribbon. They curl up like ribbons on the top of presents. Wavy hair has oval, or egg-shaped, ends. Not quite round, the strands don't lay straight in rows, like mine. Not quite flat, they don't wind and curl as much as very curly hair does.

How interesting! The more I investigate, the more new and different things I find out—right down to the hairs on our heads.

# What are fingernails and toenails for ?

Can you think of a way you are like a cat, a cow, a horse, and a hawk? I can. You have nails, and a cat has claws. Cows and horses have hoofs, and a hawk has talons.

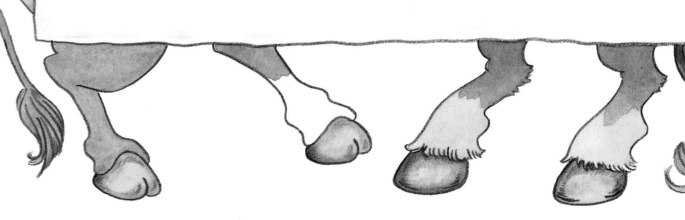

Do you see the connection? Nails, claws, talons, and hoofs are made of the same thing. It is a hard material called "keratin," which is tougher than bone. The keratin protects the animals in different ways.

Fingernails and toenails are most like claws. For millions of years, animals have used their claws for climbing and fighting for survival. Of course, people don't need claws, but hands and feet still need to be protected from getting hurt. Fingernails and toenails work nicely, like a tiny shield of armor for each finger and toe.

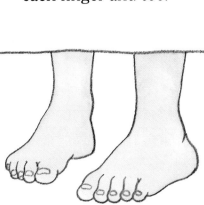

## How come you're ticklish?

Now here's a ticklish subject! Your skin comes with some excellent "detective" tools, I must say.

Tiny cells in the skin, called receptors, act like walkie-talkies. They receive "touch" messages from the outside world, such as "I am being tickled—I am being tickled!"

The skin receptors send this message to the other end of the walkie-talkie, your brain. The brain has its own special cells to send answers and commands.

When someone tickles you, the brain tells your skin to feel feathery ripples across the spot being tickled. It also sends a message to your voice box: "time to giggle—time to giggle!"

Have you ever wondered why someone can tickle you, but you cannot tickle yourself? The way I see it, tickling is a two-person game. I tickle, you giggle. You tickle, I giggle. The surprise and excitement isn't there if you try to tickle yourself, and it's just not as much fun.

# What causes goosebumps

**W**hat a scary movie! Remind me never to watch another movie with a cat in it. During the scariest parts, little bumps popped up over my body. They were goosebumps, and I wondered why they were there. Time to investigate.

Under a magnifying glass, a goosebump looks like a hill. In the middle is a hair that looks like a blade of grass. The skin is closed very tight about it. Very curious!

Now let me check my book, *Everything You Wanted to Know About Goosebumps.* It says goosebumps are a reflex—that's something your body does automatically if something happens that you cannot control. (It also says that the funny word "goosebumps" dates from a few hundred years ago, when people noticed that a freshly plucked goose had bumps that looked like the skin bumps people sometimes got.) Think of the porcupine. At times of danger, its quills stand up, ready to stick at anything that comes near. Goosebumps are *your* body's way of saying "Oh, no!" When you're cold and goosebumps form, the tight skin around each hair tries to shut out the cold. The next time you feel goosebumps, think of them as a signal your body is giving you:

"Put a sweater on!" or
"Let's get out of here!"

## Why do you blink ?

If you want to see two of my best detective tools, look at me right in the eyes. I use my eyes to spot clues.

Luckily, eyes come with some great tools—eyelids and lashes—that keep them in tip top shape. Whenever something comes too near, your eyelids quickly close. That is, you blink.

Eyelids, eyelashes, and tears all work together to keep your eyes clean. If dust gets into your eyes, you cannot see well. The eyelashes help keep dust out of your eyes. The lids blink, and tears wash the dust off the eyeballs.

Do you ever wonder why you blink so often? Well, like my bookshelves, your eyes get dusty all the time. Always tidying up a bit, your eyelids and lashes act as windshield wipers that never stop.

These plates are copyrighted by American Optical Company and are reproduced here by permission. However, these reproductions do not present true testing conditions and cannot be used as a color vision deficiency test.

# What does it mean to be color blind?

Inspectors handle all kinds of cases. Take the case of "What does it mean to be color blind?" Have you ever heard of color blindness? Here's what I found out.

When color blind people look at things, they do not see all colors. A red ball might look green, for example. In order to see all colors, eyes must have three types of seeing tools, called cones. Each type of cone sees different colors.

Color blind people are missing one or more types of cones in their eyes. These people cannot see as many colors, or mixes of colors, as others can. Some people see no color at all. Their world looks like the picture on a television set when the color fades off.

Because most color blind people have never seen some colors, they may not even realize they are color blind. Luckily, there are tests that give doctors the clues they need to help their color blind patients. You can try the experiment here, just for fun.

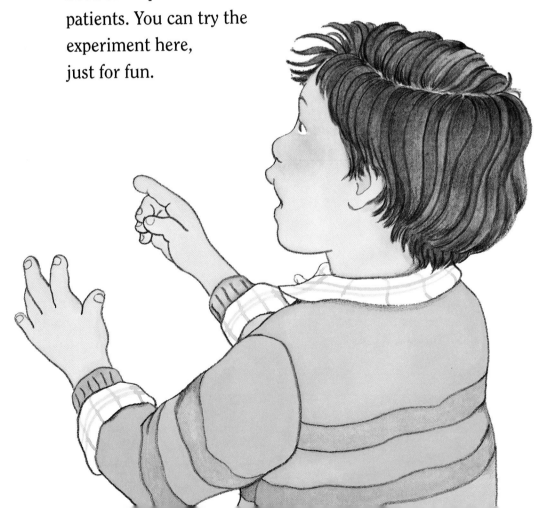

# Why do you sneeze?

**W**atch out . . . here comes a sneeze. My nose is at work again!

Like my eyes, noses can do special jobs. Not only do they sniff for clues, they protect the body in a very important way. Inside your nose, tiny hairs sway back and forth when you breathe. They stop floating bits, called particles, from going any farther into your nose. If some bits do get by, you sneeze, giving them a strong push out of your body. This way, air is clean when it reaches your lungs.

Sneezing also helps you get well. Some illnesses, like colds, cause a gluey liquid to be trapped inside the tubes between your nose and lungs. This liquid, called mucus, blocks the flow of air, and makes it hard for you to breathe. To get rid of the mucus and open your air passages, you keep sneezing.

Ker-choo! Oh no, I hope I'm not getting a cold.

# *What causes colds*

**K**er-choo! Pardon me, but I do seem to have caught a cold. I wonder how? Let me fix a cup of tea, crawl into bed, and look at my list of suspects:

Suspect number one: Cold weather. People have blamed colds on cold weather for centuries. But, come to think of it, people have colds all year round, not just when it's cold outside. Let's keep looking for suspects.

Suspect number two: Cold and wet feet, hands, or head. I always dress for the weather, but once in a while, the rain surprises me and I get soaked. Maybe I'll get a cold, or maybe not. Let's go on to the next suspect.

Suspect number three: The cold virus. Hundreds of different germs, called viruses, float in the air in tiny drops of moisture. When you breathe, some of these cold germs glide into your body. Once there, they make you sick—and they are truly guilty of causing colds. No one has discovered a cure for the common cold. You can be certain, though, that we inspectors will be on the case until a cure is found.

# Why do you sleep?

Shhh. My friend the beaver is very busy, as usual. But he's just sleeping, you say? Listen, as an inspector, I know that things are not always what they seem. Actually, all of us work on some very important projects when we sleep.

Many scientists think that as you snuggle and snooze, parts of your body are still at work. For instance, the cells in your bones and muscles multiply, or make more and more of themselves. So every night, while you still are young, your body grows taller, bigger, and stronger.

Scientists also think that sleep helps to make you better if you are sick. When you're awake, you use energy to move about, think, talk, and play. Because you are not moving much when you sleep, your body can use its energy to strengthen armies of cells that fight germs. Germs are "invader" cells from outside the body and they can make you sick.

Like the other cells, the germ-fighters multiply each night, making sure you have a fresh supply whenever you need them.

Sleep on, Beaver, and keep up the good work!

# *What causes dreams*

Your brain stays busy when you sleep. As the thinking part of your body, it makes weird and wacky "movies" inside your head each night, called dreams. Maybe you don't remember the dreams, but they are there.

Whether they are scary or funny, your dreams are important. Many scientists believe they let your brain work on problems or projects during sleep. In fact, some people even get good ideas from their dreams. Maybe you will dream about a character, and then be able to make up a good story that came to you in your dream.

Scientists think that dreaming even seems to sharpen the mind. If people wake up before they have enough time to dream, they do not think or learn as well when they are awake that day.

Yawwwwn. Well, I think it's about bedtime. Maybe I can help solve some important cases tonight while I dream!

31

Anytime you have a question about how your body works, just ask. After all, the more you know about your body, the better you can take care of yourself.

Get into the habit of asking questions and searching for answers, on any subject. That's how Inspector McQ works. You can, too.

## To Parents

Children love to ask questions. *All About You*, with special "mouse detective" McQ, will provide your child with the answers to many common questions children ask about themselves. These answers will serve as a bridge into learning some important concepts. Here are a few easy and natural ways your child can express feelings and understandings about what Inspector McQ has to say. You know your child and can best judge which ideas he or she will enjoy most.

Gather several pictures of your child at different ages. Help your child put the pictures in order from youngest to oldest. Then talk about how your child has grown and changed from year to year. Some things you can discuss are your child's changing size and shape, as well as eye color and hair color and length. See how these features compare with those of other family members or friends.

Talk with your child about scary things that might cause goosebumps. Help explain why some things are scary because they are dangerous, while other things, like some stories, are scary but fun. Encourage your child to tell

you a scary story. Make sure to say whenever you get "goosebumps."

Talk with your child about animals that have claws, like cats and dogs. How do the animals use their claws? How do they sharpen them or wear them down? Then talk about fingernails and toenails. How are they different from claws? How do people use their fingernails and toenails?

Pick any section of the book to read again with your child. Then help your child put together a poster with information from that section. For example, a poster called "Stop Colds" will be a useful reminder of things we can do to keep from catching a cold.